Early Civilizations of the Americas

Rosie McCormick

CoreKnowledge

ISBN: 978-1-68380-406-2

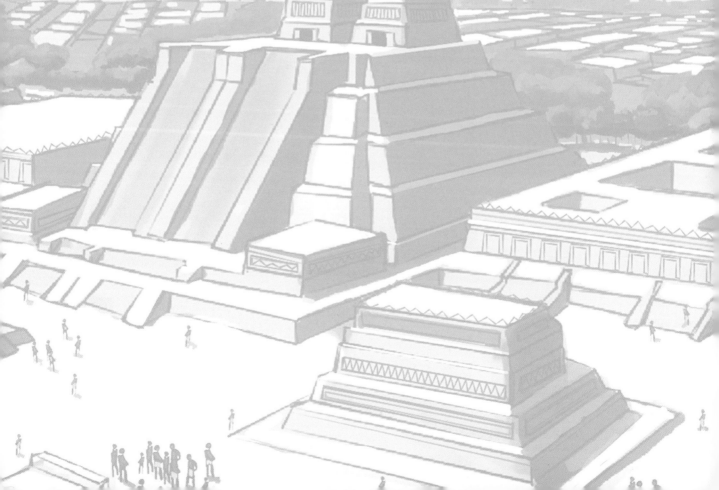

Early Civilizations of the Americas

Table of Contents

Hunters and Gatherers

Long, long ago people all over the world found food by hunting and gathering. This meant they moved from place to place as they followed animals and

gathered plants, nuts, and berries. Some people walked great distances hunting and gathering as they went. Others traveled in small boats, following the coastlines until they found a place to hunt and gather.

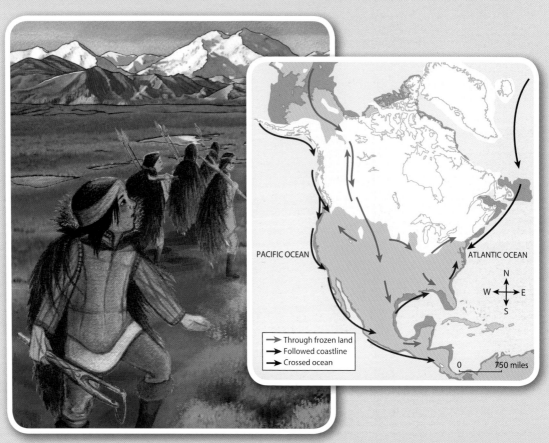

Some of the people who had found themselves in North America followed herds of large animals known as woolly mammoths. Woolly mammoths looked like African elephants, though their ears were smaller and their tusks were longer!

Animals such as woolly mammoths not only provided these people with food, they also gave them fur, skin, and bones that were used to make clothing, tools, and simple, warm homes.

At certain times of the year across North America, people were able to gather fruits, berries, and plants. They used these foods during the winter months.

They even gathered a sweet syrup from the trees in the forests and woodlands. And they fished in the oceans, rivers, and streams too!

From Hunting to Farming

Over many years people kept on moving across North America. This movement of people also happened in Central and South America. Then there came a time when some people became quite good at farming.

They took wild plants that they had eaten for hundreds of years, and by experimenting with these plants, they developed a new crop called corn.

The development of farming created more food for people to eat. This meant that more people could live in one place. Some people continued to travel in search of food. But many settled and stayed in places where they could raise food crops and hunt on land near their farms.

The Marvelous Maya

The Maya were one of several groups of people who lived and farmed in the Americas. The Maya became expert farmers. They made canals, or channels dug into the earth, to carry water to areas of farmland that were dry. They farmed on mountainsides and in the forests. They hunted and fished too.

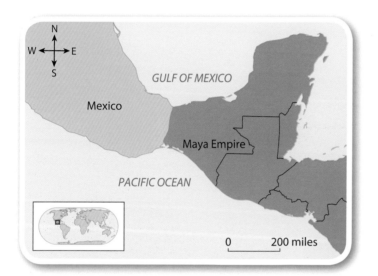

Successful farming led to the growth of a great Maya civilization. The Maya built great cities. The cities and their surrounding lands were ruled by kings and queens. Farmers grew the crops that fed the increasing Maya population.

The Maya built pyramids that were used to worship their gods. They believed their gods controlled the world. For example, the Maya believed in a god of mountains and earthquakes, a god of thunder, and a god of the sky. Maya priests were in charge of the many religious ceremonies that were part of everyday life.

Maya priests were also doctors and astronomers. The astronomer priests carefully watched the movements of the stars. They learned about the movement of the sun and the changing of the seasons. The Maya did this without any tools or instruments, just with the naked eye!

By studying the night sky, the Maya priests were able to create a calendar that recorded the change of the seasons, and the number of days in a year. The Maya came up with 365 days too! Maya farmers used the calendar to tell them when to plant and harvest their crops. They also planned their celebrations around this calendar!

The Maya developed a number system made up of lines, circles, dots, and ovals. Numbers were used to record information about such things as crops and goods.

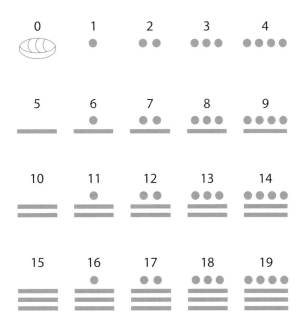

The Maya also had a system of writing made up of symbols called glyphs. The sons and some daughters of important people learned to read and write. When they were older, some became scribes and wrote down important information on paper made from tree bark. They also carved messages on stone walls and on buildings.

The Maya played a popular ball game. The game had a different name depending on where it was played. Almost every Maya city had a ball court as big as a modern football field. The ball used in this game was a heavy, rubber ball. Players had to keep the ball in the air using only their knees, hips, shoulders, and forearms. Players scored points by passing the ball through stone hoops. The team with the most points won.

CHAPTER
4

The Amazing Aztec

Hundreds of years ago, in
the Americas, a group of
people set off in search
of a home. These people
became the creators of
the Aztec Empire. As the
story goes, the Aztec
believed that their sun

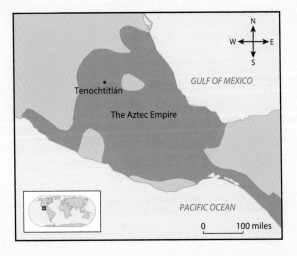

god had told them to search for an eagle eating a snake,
while sitting on a prickly pear cactus. When they found
such a thing, they were to settle in that place.

According to the story, they found an island in the middle of a beautiful lake in central Mexico. And on the island they spotted an eagle perched on a cactus—and yes, it was eating a snake! It was on

that island that the Aztec built the most amazing city called Tenochtitlán, which means "the place of the prickly pear." The island and the city are now modern-day Mexico City.

This is the modern flag of Mexico. On it you can see the eagle, the snake, and the cactus. This Aztec story is an important part of Mexican culture.

The Aztec built bridges from their island city to the shore of the lake. Because the lake contained salt water, the Aztec used clay pipes to bring in fresh water from the mainland nearby. The water was used for drinking and cooking.

They built canals, or waterways, and moved about the city in canoes. They farmed on the island too by creating gardens on raised beds. The Aztec did this by digging up mud from the bottom of the lake and piling it up. Then they shaped the piles into long, narrow gardens and planted such crops as maize, beans, and squash. They also grew flowers.

Tenochtitlán also had streets and tall buildings. At the very center of the city was the Great Temple. The Aztec emperor, or ruler, and the priests who were in charge of all religious practices lived in grand palaces in the city. The Aztec believed in many gods, but the sun god and the rain god were among the most important. The Great Temple was used for the worship of Aztec gods.

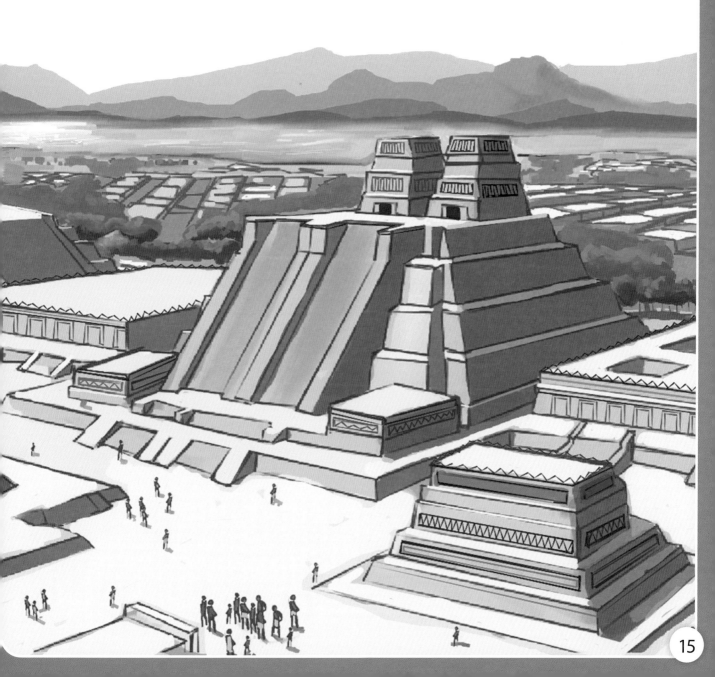

More than two hundred thousand people lived in the city of Tenochtitlán. It was one of the biggest cities in the world at the time. The city had busy marketplaces where many people traded

goods. Farmers brought their food crops to the city from the gardens and fields nearby. They traded food crops for things they needed. People also traded gold and silver jewelry, tools, clay pots, clothing, feathers, and seashells.

The Aztec were strong and skillful warriors. They conquered other people and took their land. They created an empire. The Aztec emperor was the most powerful person in the empire. One of the greatest Aztec emperors was Moctezuma II. He was so powerful, when he entered a room, people threw themselves on the floor.

Some Aztec boys learned to read and write. The priests were their teachers. Some were also taught medicine and astronomy. Others learned to be craftsmen or farmers. All boys trained from an early age to be warriors. Girls learned other skills, including pottery and weaving.

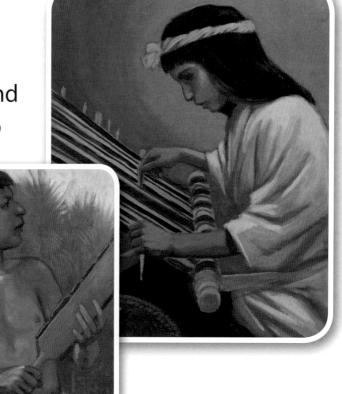

The Incredible Inca

The Aztec created a great empire, but the Inca built an even bigger one that stretched all along the western coast of South America. Today that empire would include large parts of the modern-day countries of Peru, Colombia,

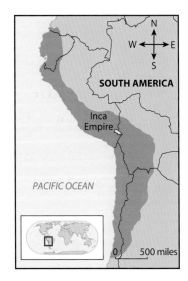

Ecuador, Bolivia, Chile, and Argentina. At the head of this amazing empire, the man in charge of millions of people, was the all-powerful Sapa Inca.

The Inca were expert road builders. They built a road called the Royal Road, which stretched for two thousand miles. For a time it was the longest road in the world. Inca soldiers could move quickly along the road if they were needed. And farmers could easily move from place to place to trade their crops, which included cocoa and many different kinds of potatoes.

The Inca also used a chain of speedy messengers who ran along the Royal Road taking important news from place to place. The Inca did not have a written language, so each runner had to remember their message so they could tell it to the next runner.

However, the Inca did have their own way of counting and recording information. They used a quipu. A quipu was a group of different colored strings with knots tied in a certain way. The strings and knots might show numbers of soldiers, or give information about farmers' crops.

Like the Maya and the Aztec, the Inca worshipped different gods. Of special importance to them was the sun god. Here, the Inca sun god is shown wearing the sun as his crown. He is also shown crying precious raindrops, which is a sign that he has the power to bring rain to the farmers' crops. The sun god holds a thunderbolt in his hand to show his strength and power!

The Inca also built great cities with temples and palaces. Perhaps one of the most remarkable cities ever built is the Inca city of Machu Picchu, which sits high up in the Andes Mountains of modern-day Peru. The stones used to build the city were so carefully cut that they fit together like jigsaw pieces. The city was built for a powerful Inca king.

A Story from the Americas

The people of these early civilizations often wondered how the world was created, or made. Their religions helped them to make sense of this mystery and, for some, provided answers. The Maya had their own story about the creation of Earth. Maya storytellers passed this story from one generation to the next— all the way down to today. This is the Maya story of how Earth and its people came to be.

In the beginning there was no Earth. There was only darkness. But then the gods created a place between the sea and the sky. This happened when two of the gods, Tepew and Q'uk'umatz, shouted out the name "Earth." Suddenly Earth appeared. Mountains rose up, and plains appeared. Trees and plants grew across the land.

However, Earth was silent until the gods filled it with animals of every kind. Suddenly there were jaguars, pumas, snakes, deer, and antelope on the land. The gods filled the oceans with animals too.

But soon the gods realized that they needed people. They began by making clay people. The clay people looked good, but they could not move. They could not walk about. And when the sun shone bright, they began to melt!

The gods knew they must start again. So they decided to make wooden people. The wooden people were stronger. They did not melt in the warm sun. But the wooden people were not quite right. For one thing, they could not think for themselves.

The gods tried one last time to create the people they wanted to live on Earth. They asked the animals to help them. The animals showed the gods a perfect place for people to live. In this place grew yellow and white corn. The gods created humans from that corn.

The first humans could hear, see, and think. The humans thanked the gods and built great temples in their honor. These humans were exactly what the gods had hoped for, and they were happy.

The Maya, Aztec, and Inca Today

At least six million Maya still live in Central America. Many speak the languages of their ancestors, follow their traditions, and, as you have

heard, listen to their stories. They weave cloth, grow the same crops, and eat the same food. But they also go to school, watch TV, and play games just like you do!

In Mexico, descendants of the Aztec enjoy celebrating their culture. Many people speak Nahuatl, the language of the people who made their home on the island in the lake. They perform Aztec dances and wear traditional dress. And just as their ancestors did, the Aztec people of today love flowers, which are a big part of their holidays and celebrations.

If you were to travel up into the Andes Mountains of Peru, you would meet the descendants of the Inca. You would meet people in brightly colored clothing walking on mountain paths with llamas at their side. You would hear Quechua, the language of the people who built Machu Picchu. You would most likely be invited to taste the different kinds of potatoes that the Inca people love to eat. And you would be able to watch the sun set over the beautiful Andes Mountains.

CKHG™

Core Knowledge HISTORY AND GEOGRAPHY™

Editorial Directors

Linda Bevilacqua and Rosie McCormick

Subject Matter Expert

Jeffrey Hantman, PhD, Department of Anthropology, University of Virginia

Illustration and Photo Credits